Life

takes you unexpected

places **love**

brings you

home

from: _____

date: _____

MY JOURNAL

Belongs to:

_____

_____

Location:

_____

Date:

_____

HAPPENINGS

EXPERIENCES

THOUGHTS

HAPPENINGS

EXPERIENCES

THOUGHTS

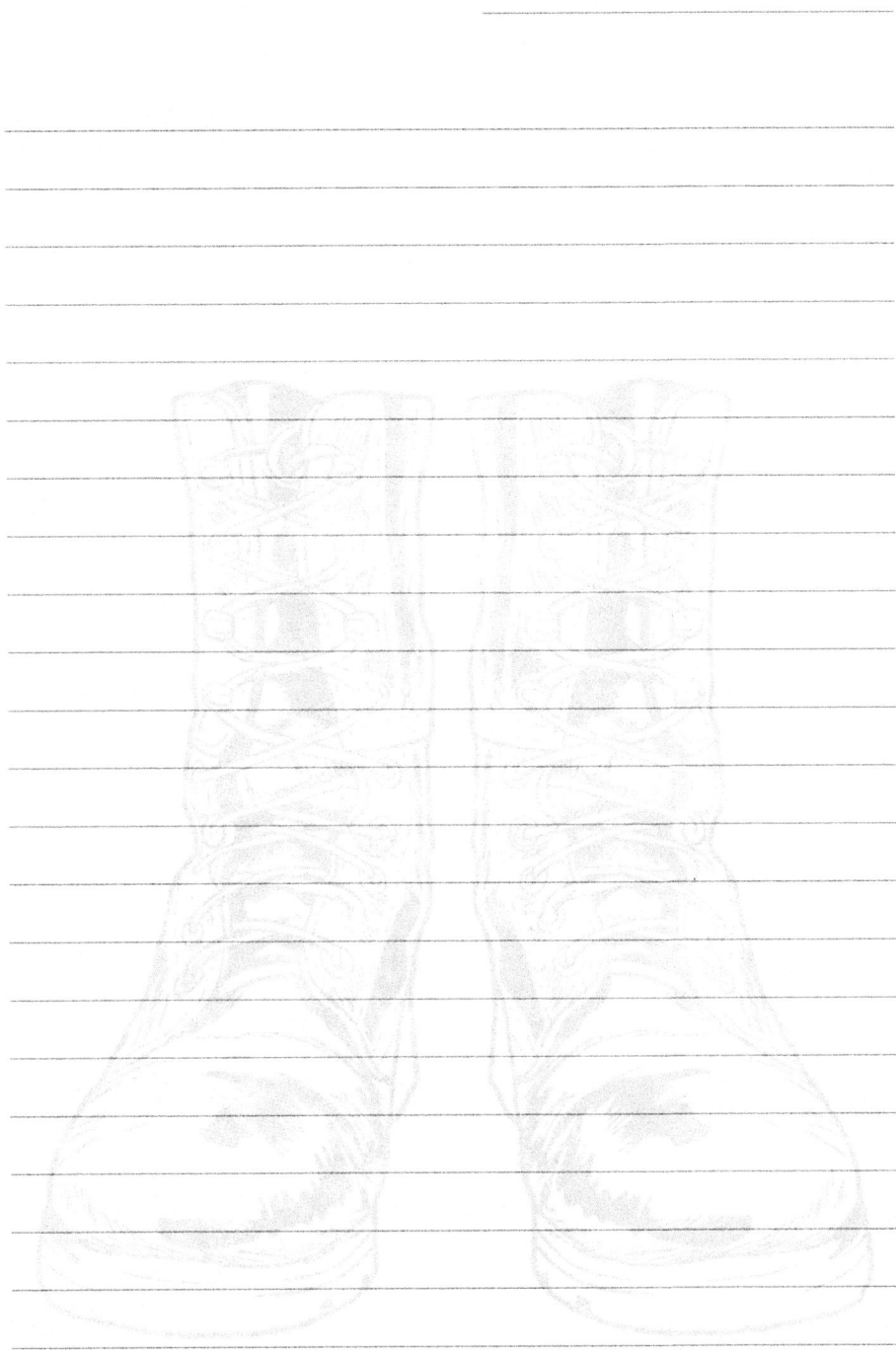

HAPPENINGS

EXPERIENCES

THOUGHTS

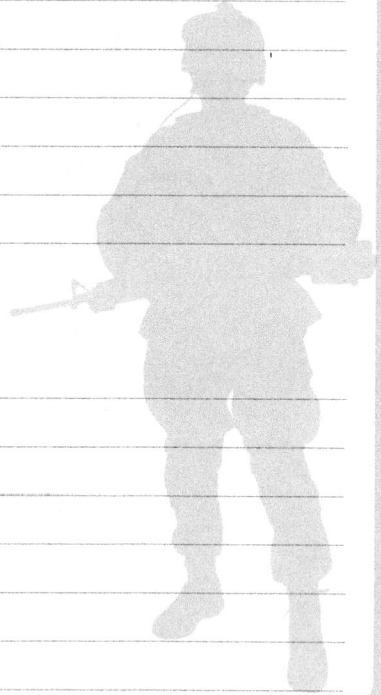

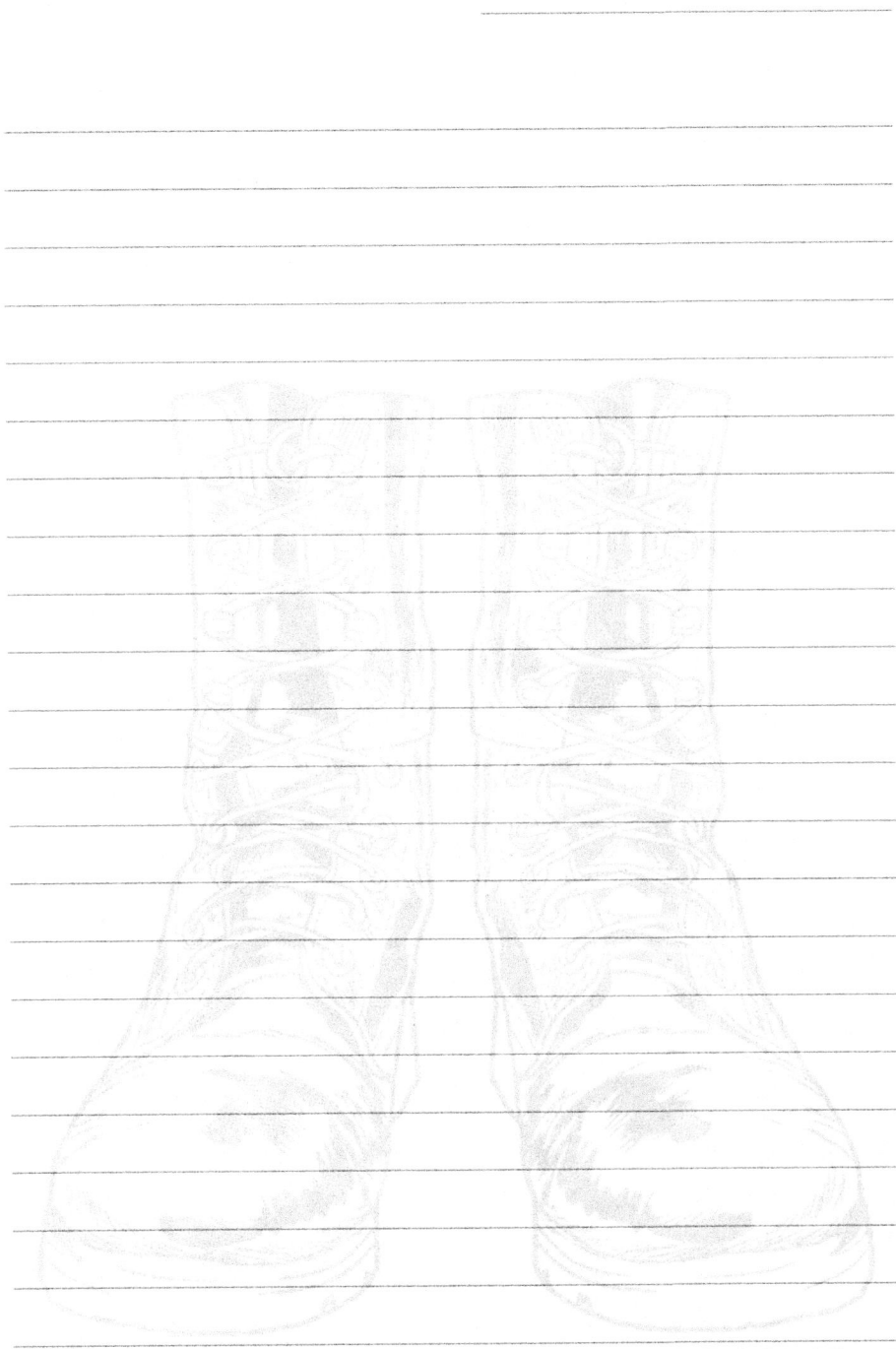

HAPPENINGS

EXPERIENCES

THOUGHTS

HAPPENINGS

EXPERIENCES

THOUGHTS

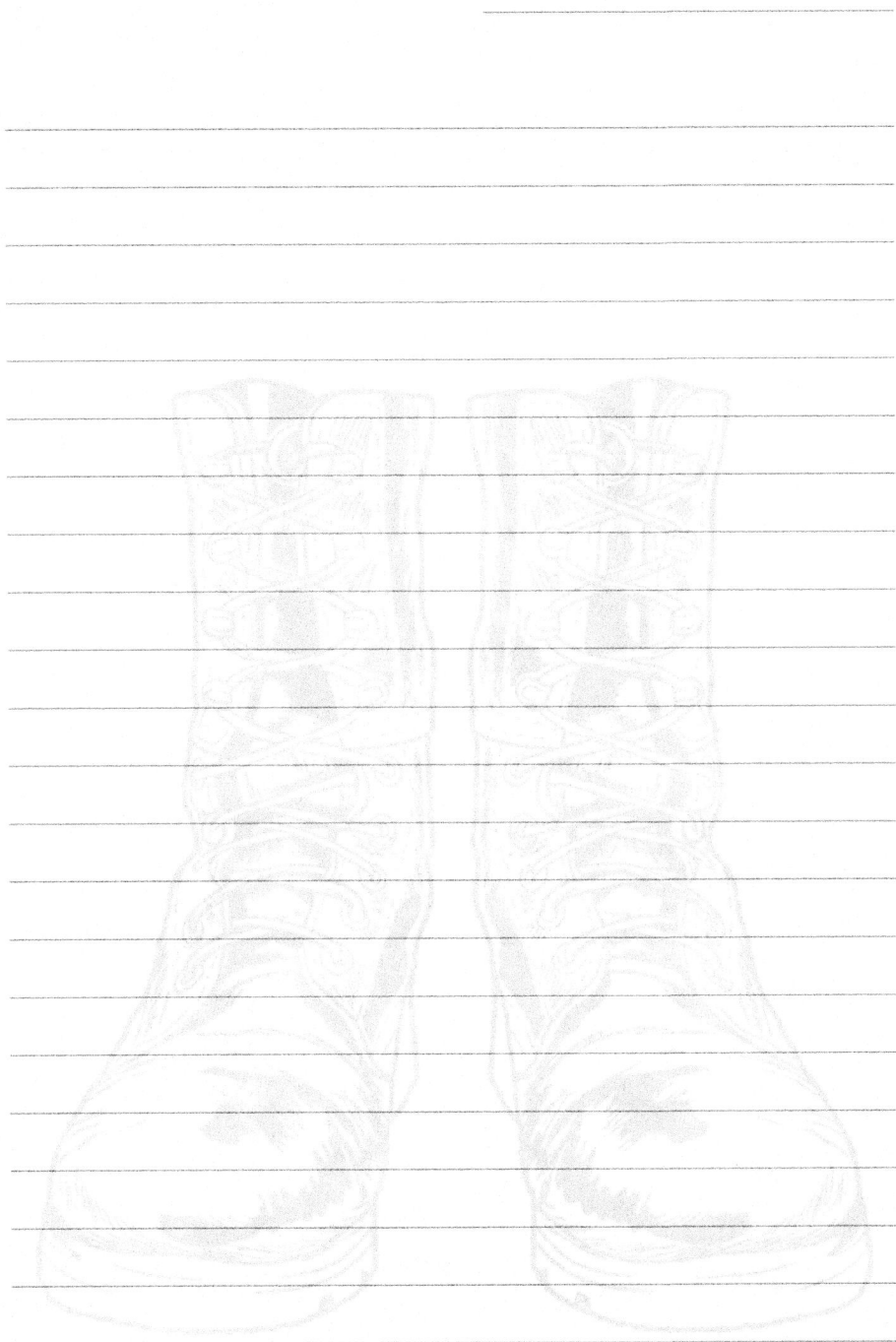

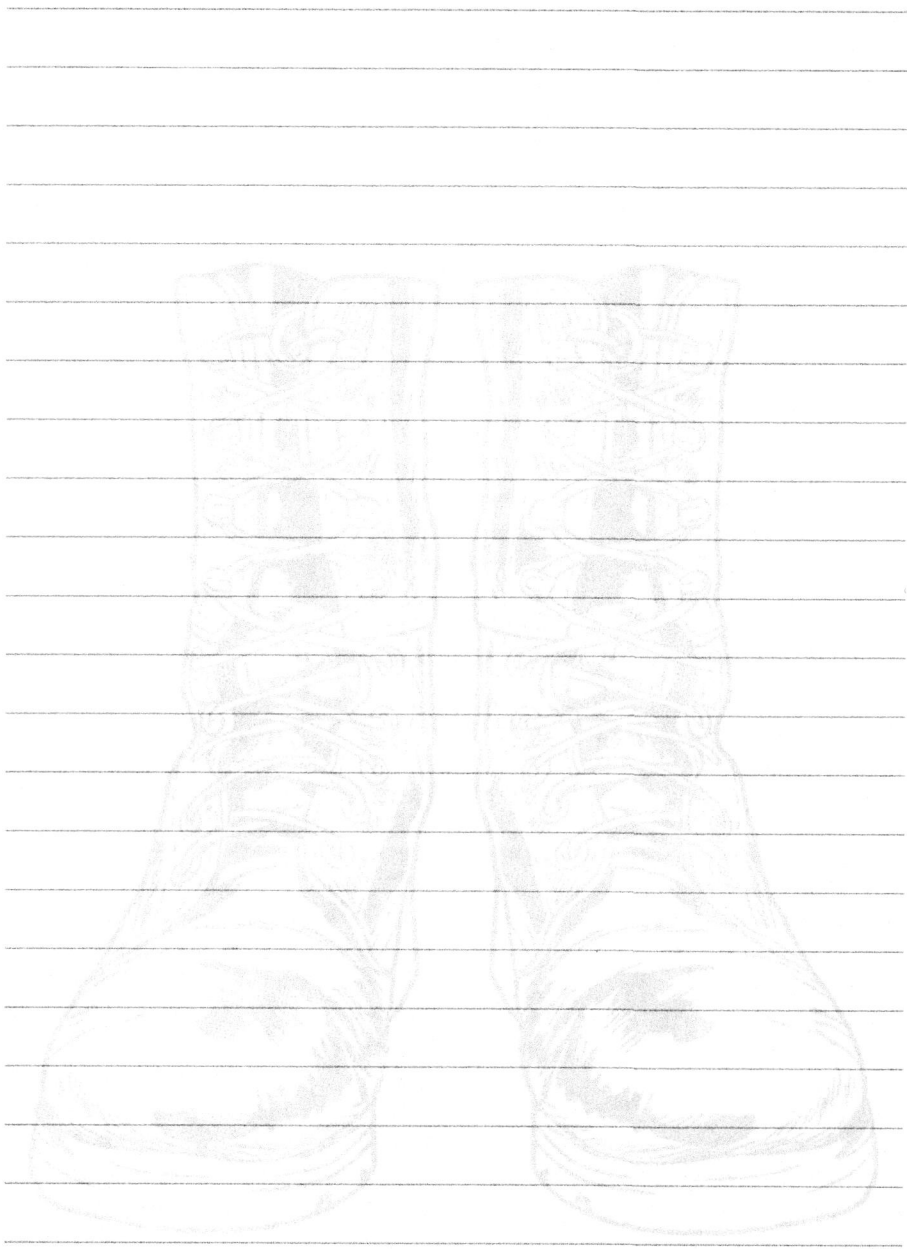

HAPPENINGS

_____
_____
_____
_____
_____
_____
_____

EXPERIENCES

_____
_____
_____
_____
_____
_____

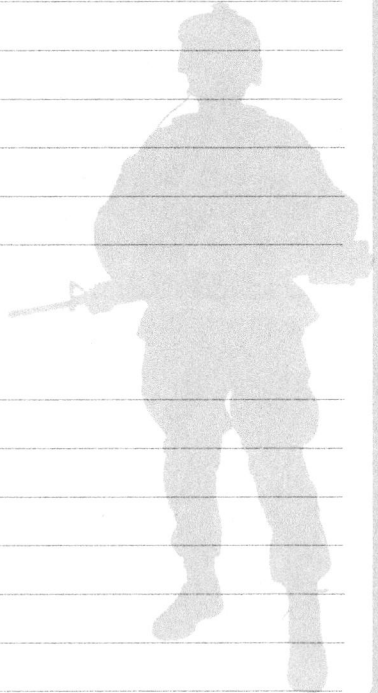

THOUGHTS

_____
_____
_____
_____
_____
_____
_____

HAPPENINGS

EXPERIENCES

THOUGHTS

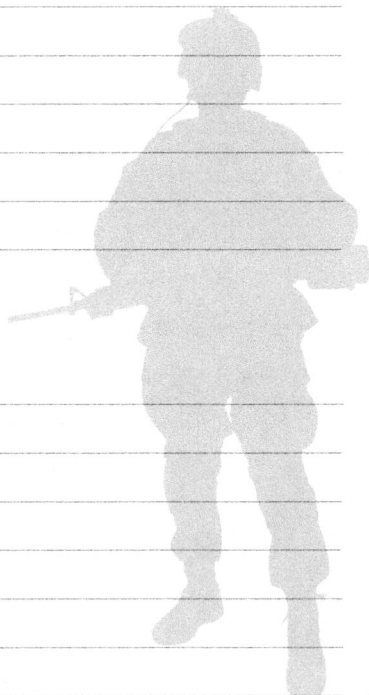

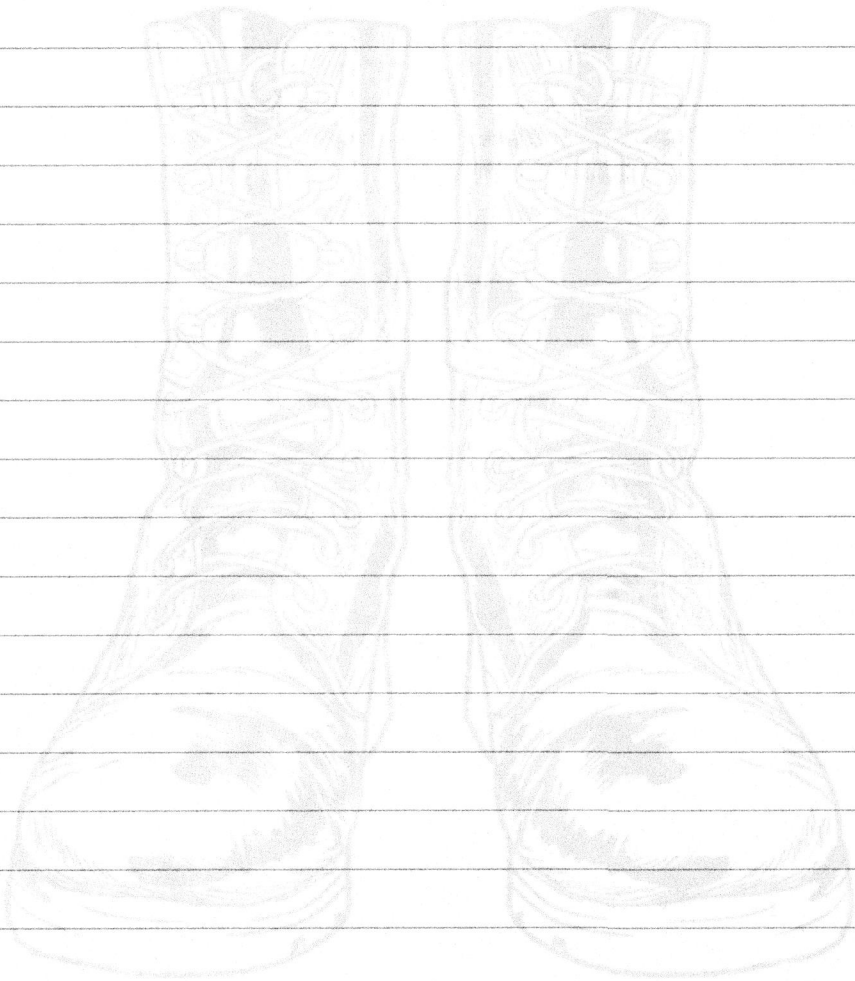

HAPPENINGS

EXPERIENCES

THOUGHTS

HAPPENINGS

EXPERIENCES

THOUGHTS

HAPPENINGS

EXPERIENCES

THOUGHTS

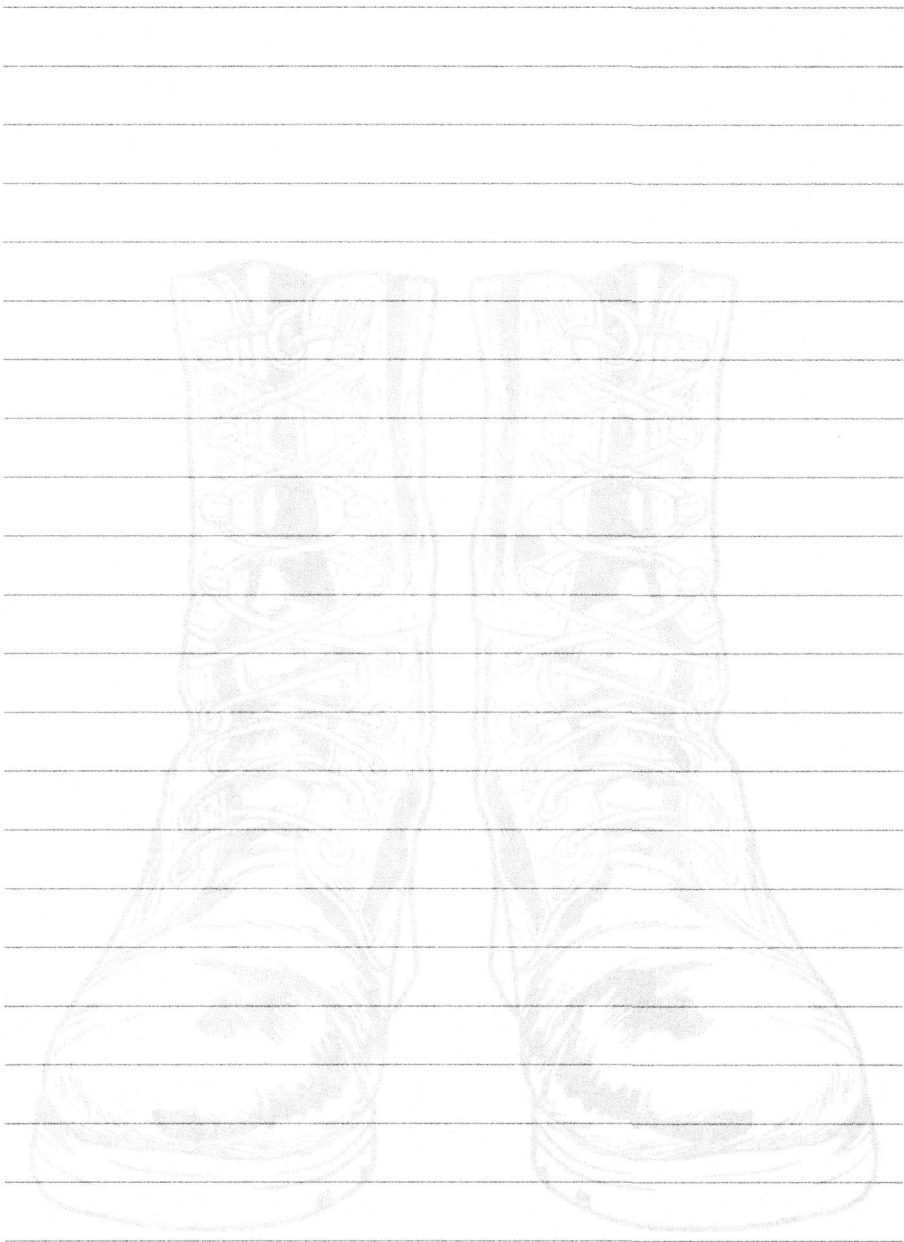

HAPPENINGS

EXPERIENCES

THOUGHTS

HAPPENINGS

EXPERIENCES

THOUGHTS

HAPPENINGS

_____
_____
_____
_____
_____
_____

EXPERIENCES

_____
_____
_____
_____
_____
_____

THOUGHTS

_____
_____
_____
_____
_____
_____
_____

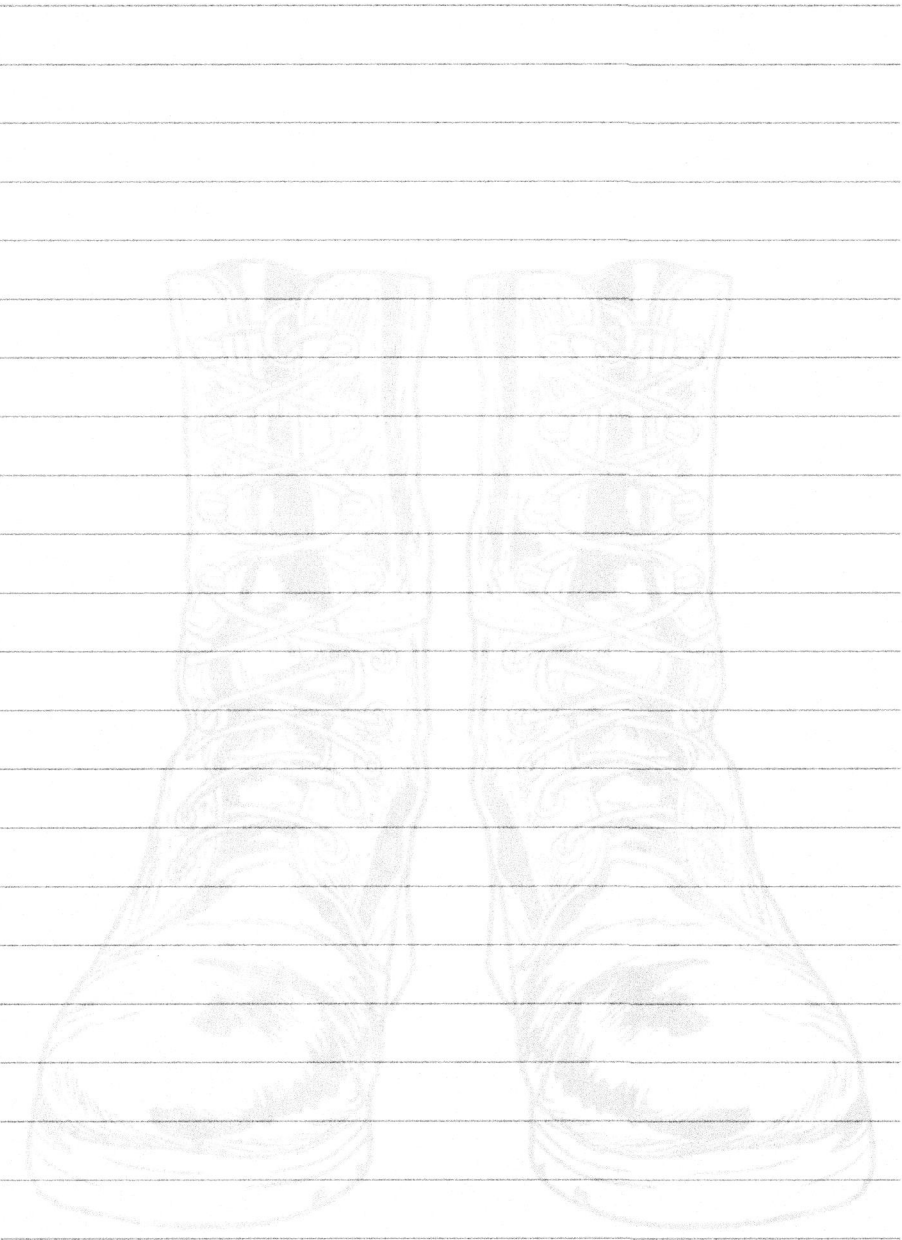

HAPPENINGS

EXPERIENCES

THOUGHTS

HAPPENINGS

EXPERIENCES

THOUGHTS

HAPPENINGS

EXPERIENCES

THOUGHTS

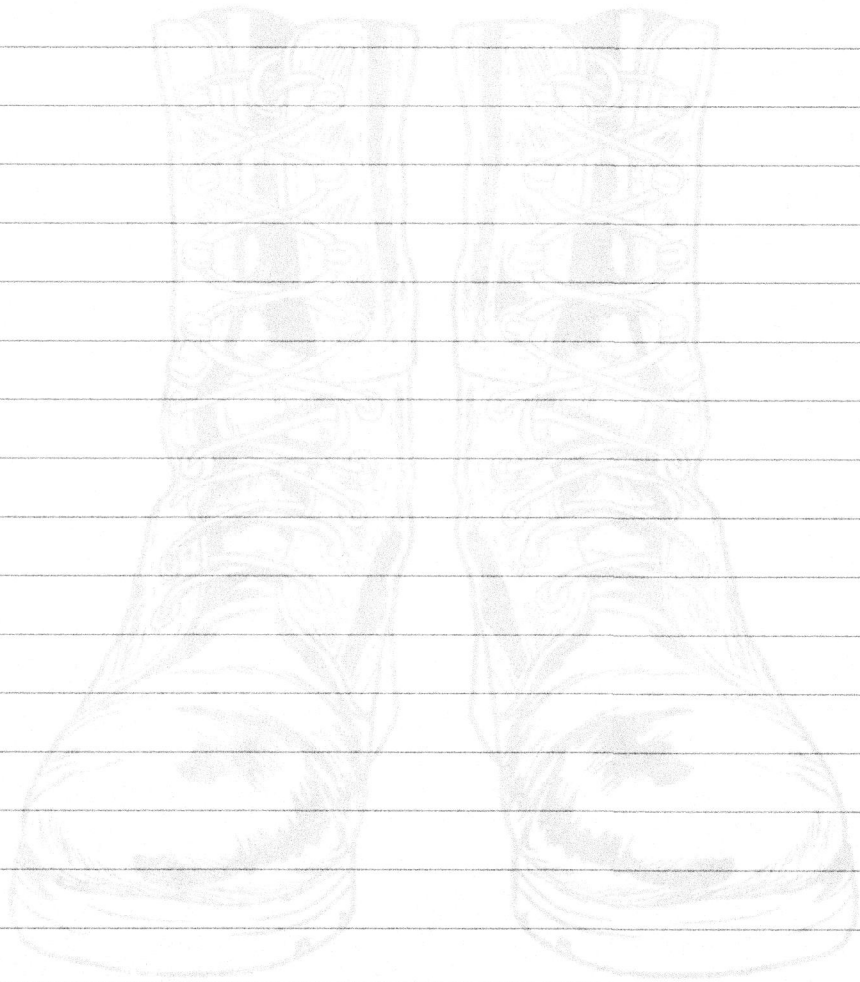

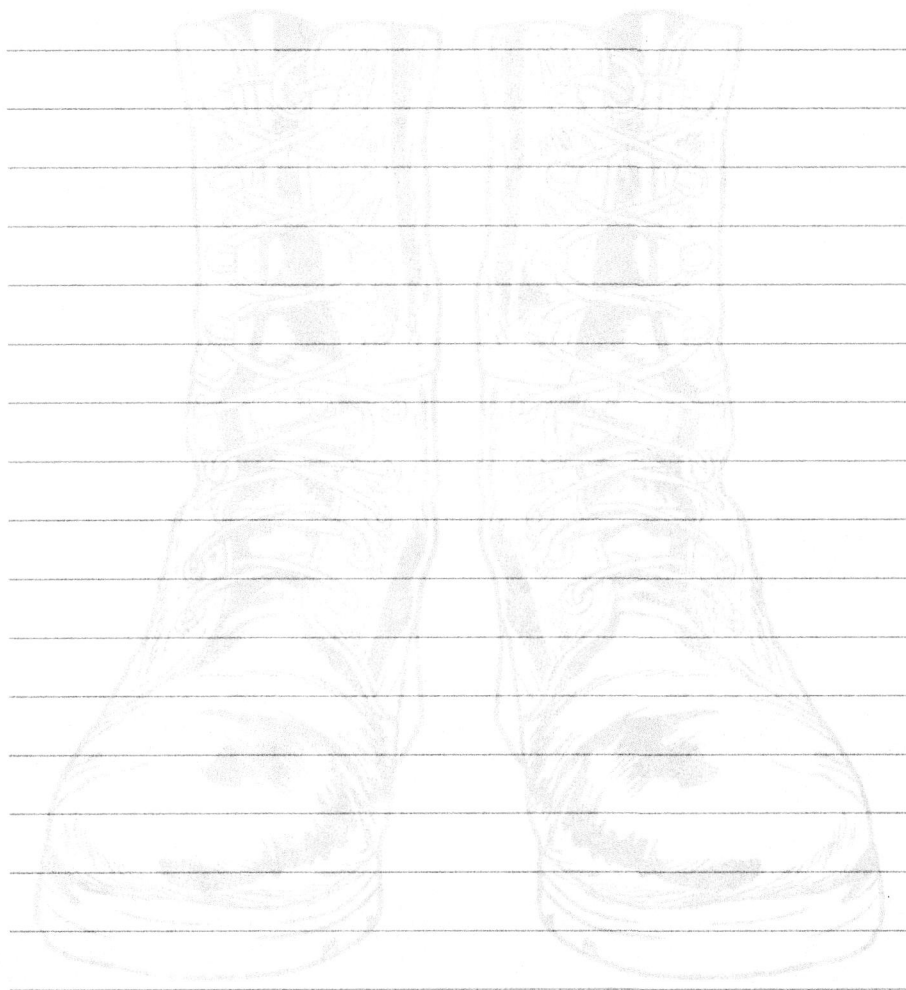

HAPPENINGS

_____
_____
_____
_____
_____
_____
_____

EXPERIENCES

_____
_____
_____
_____
_____
_____
_____

THOUGHTS

_____
_____
_____
_____
_____
_____
_____
_____

HAPPENINGS

_____
_____
_____
_____
_____
_____

EXPERIENCES

_____
_____
_____
_____
_____
_____

THOUGHTS

_____
_____
_____
_____
_____
_____
_____

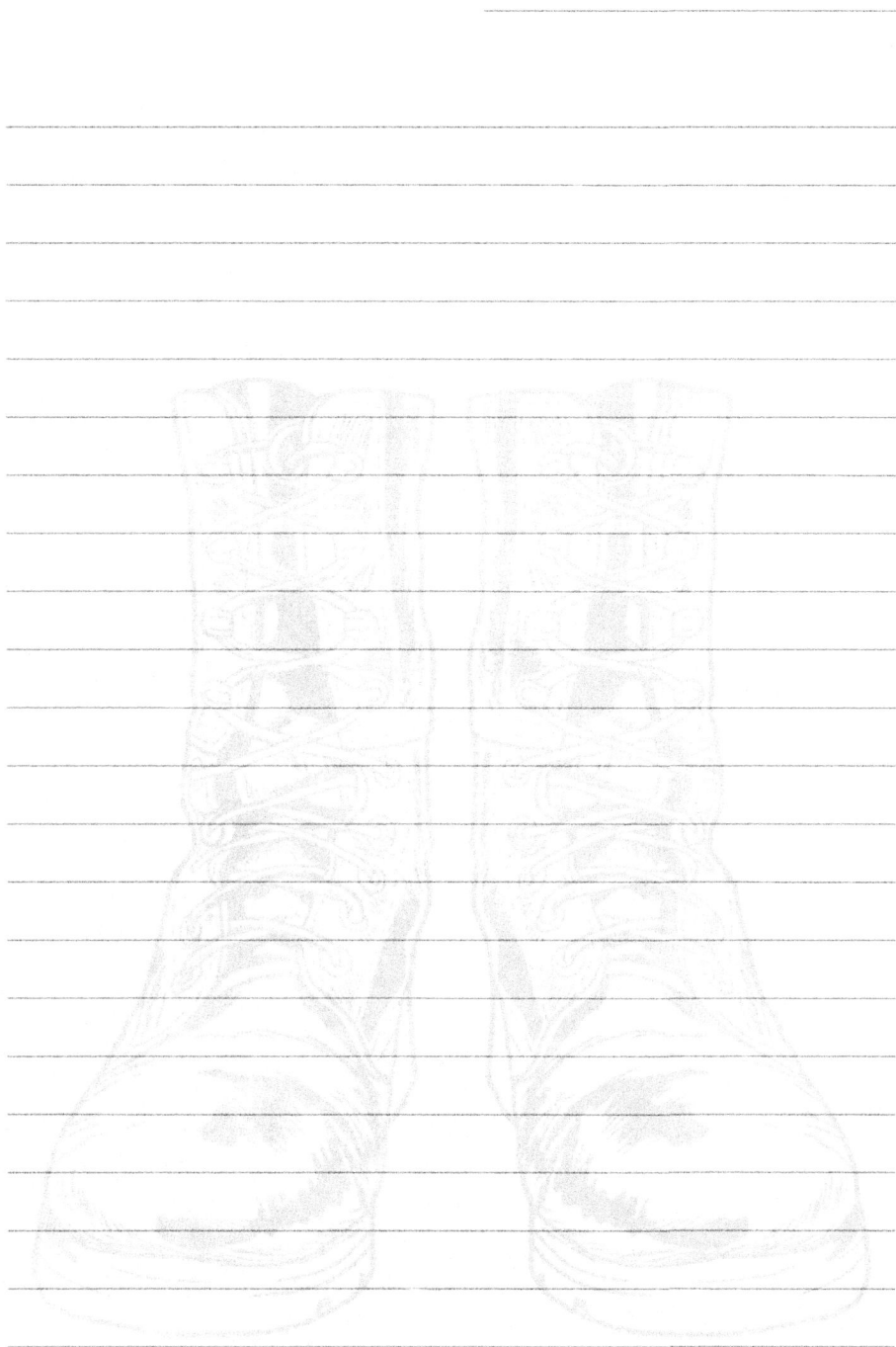

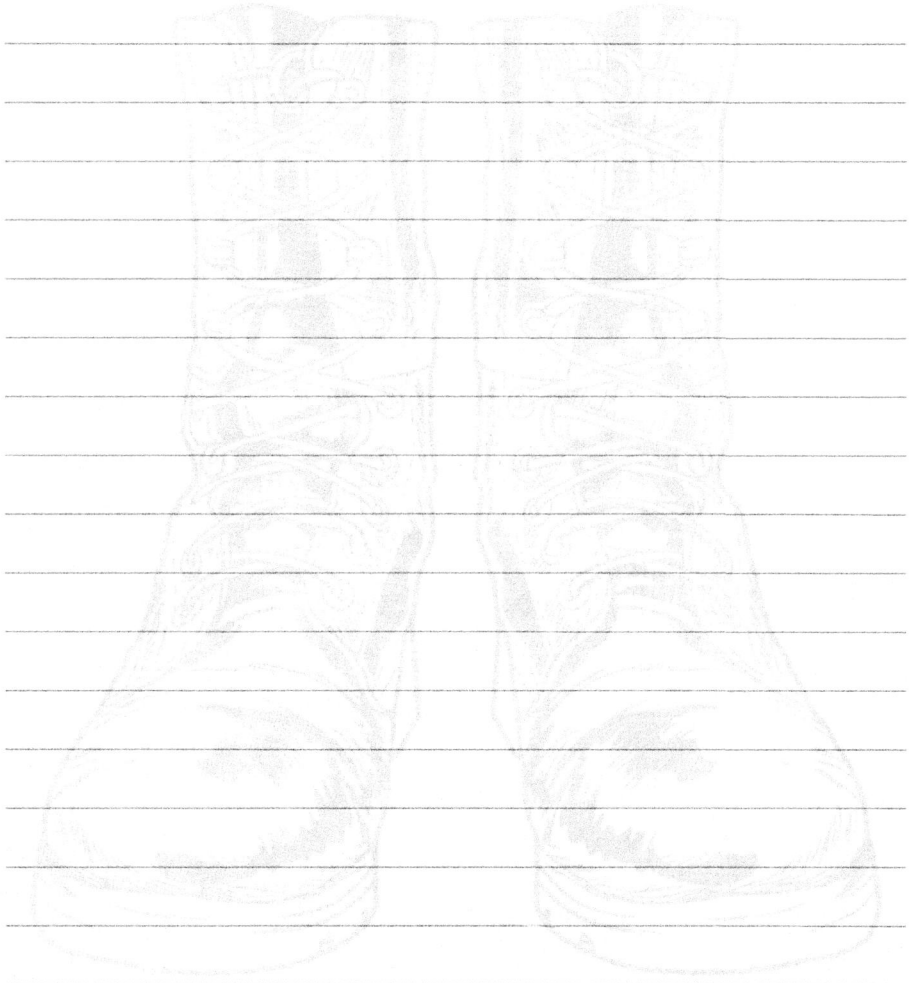

HAPPENINGS

EXPERIENCES

THOUGHTS

HAPPENINGS

EXPERIENCES

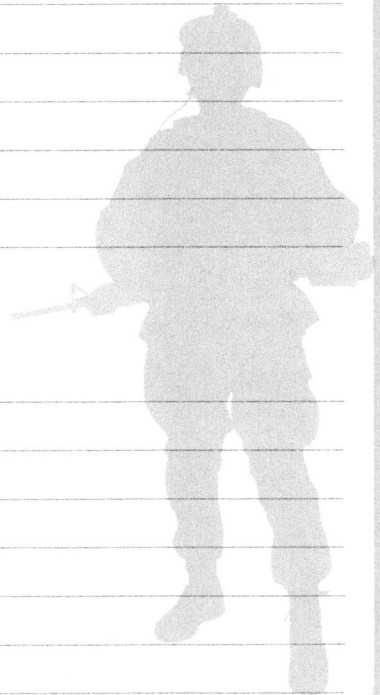

THOUGHTS

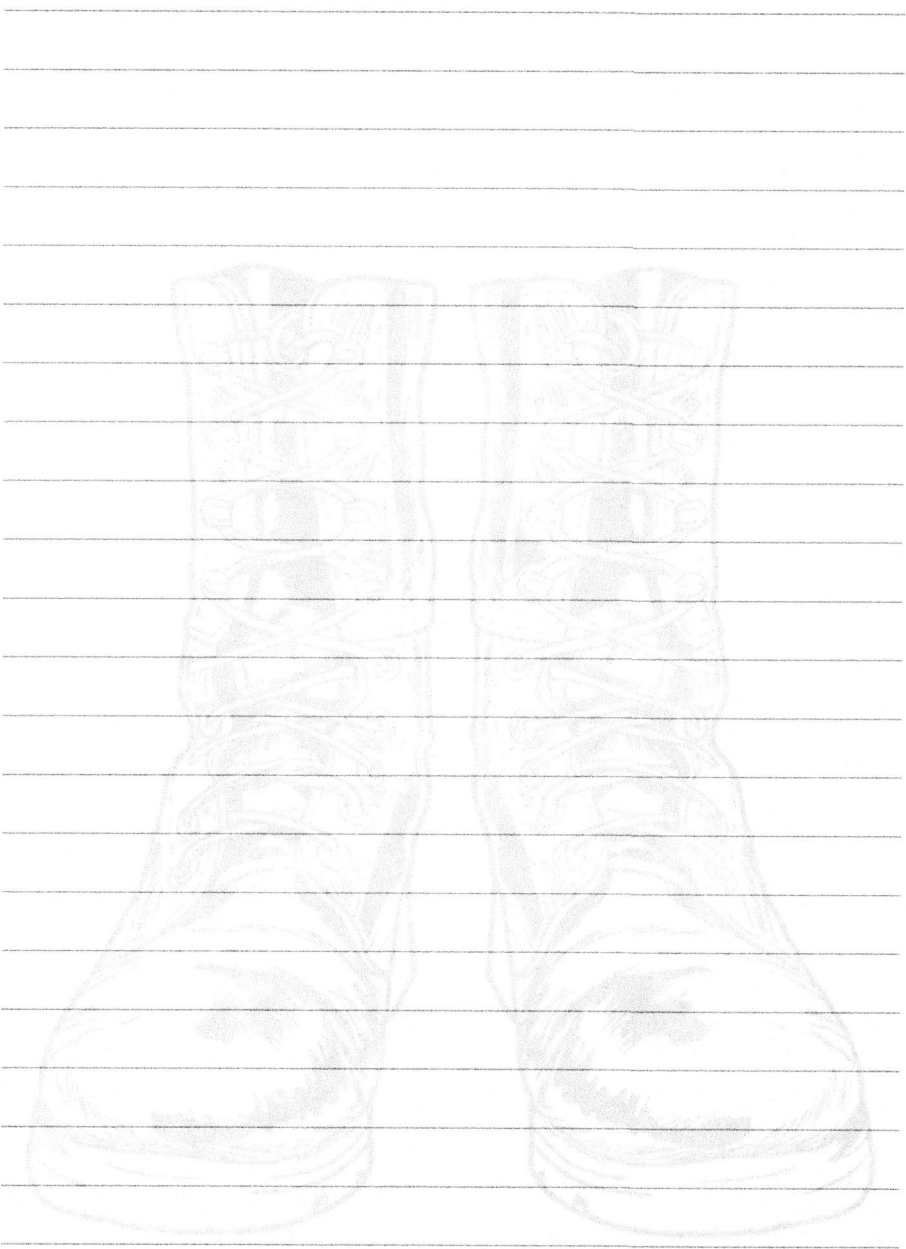

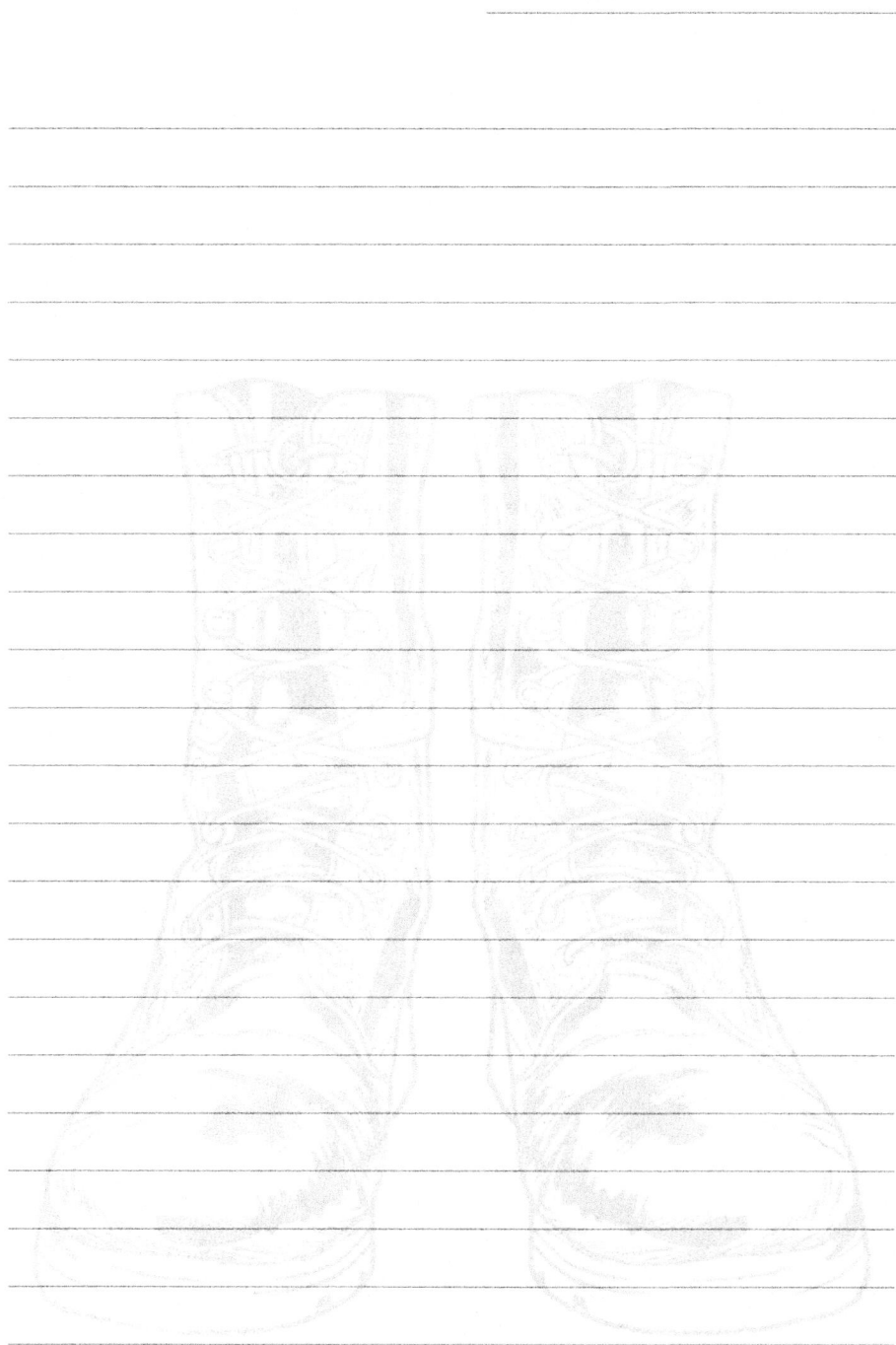

HAPPENINGS

_____
_____
_____
_____
_____
_____

EXPERIENCES

_____
_____
_____
_____
_____
_____

THOUGHTS

_____
_____
_____
_____
_____
_____
_____

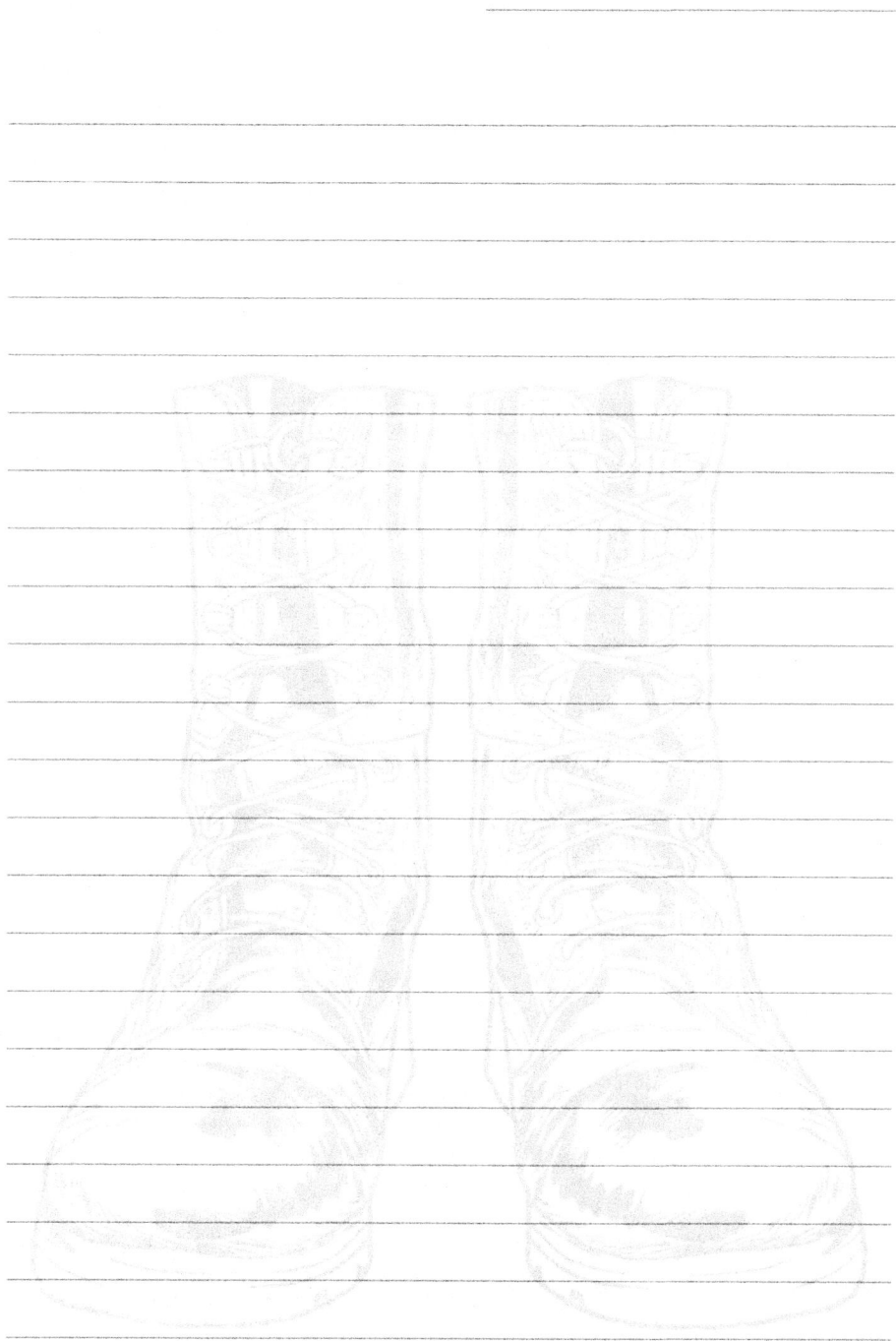

HAPPENINGS

_____
_____
_____
_____
_____
_____
_____

EXPERIENCES

_____
_____
_____
_____
_____
_____

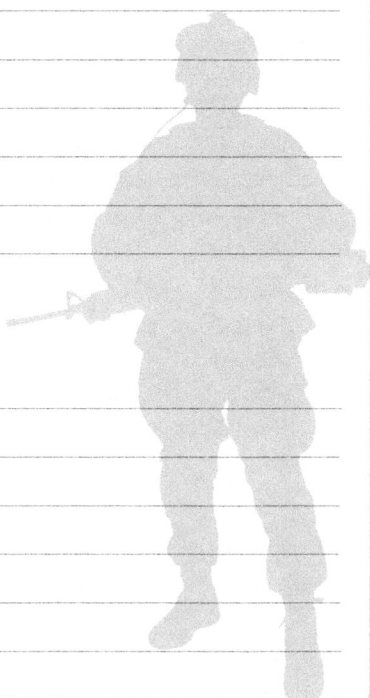

THOUGHTS

_____
_____
_____
_____
_____
_____
_____

HAPPENINGS

EXPERIENCES

THOUGHTS

HAPPENINGS

EXPERIENCES

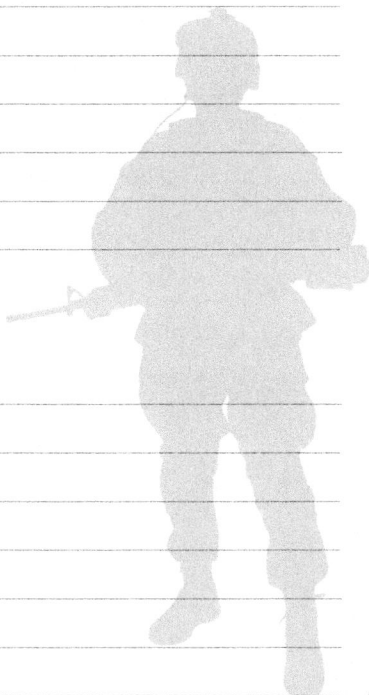

THOUGHTS

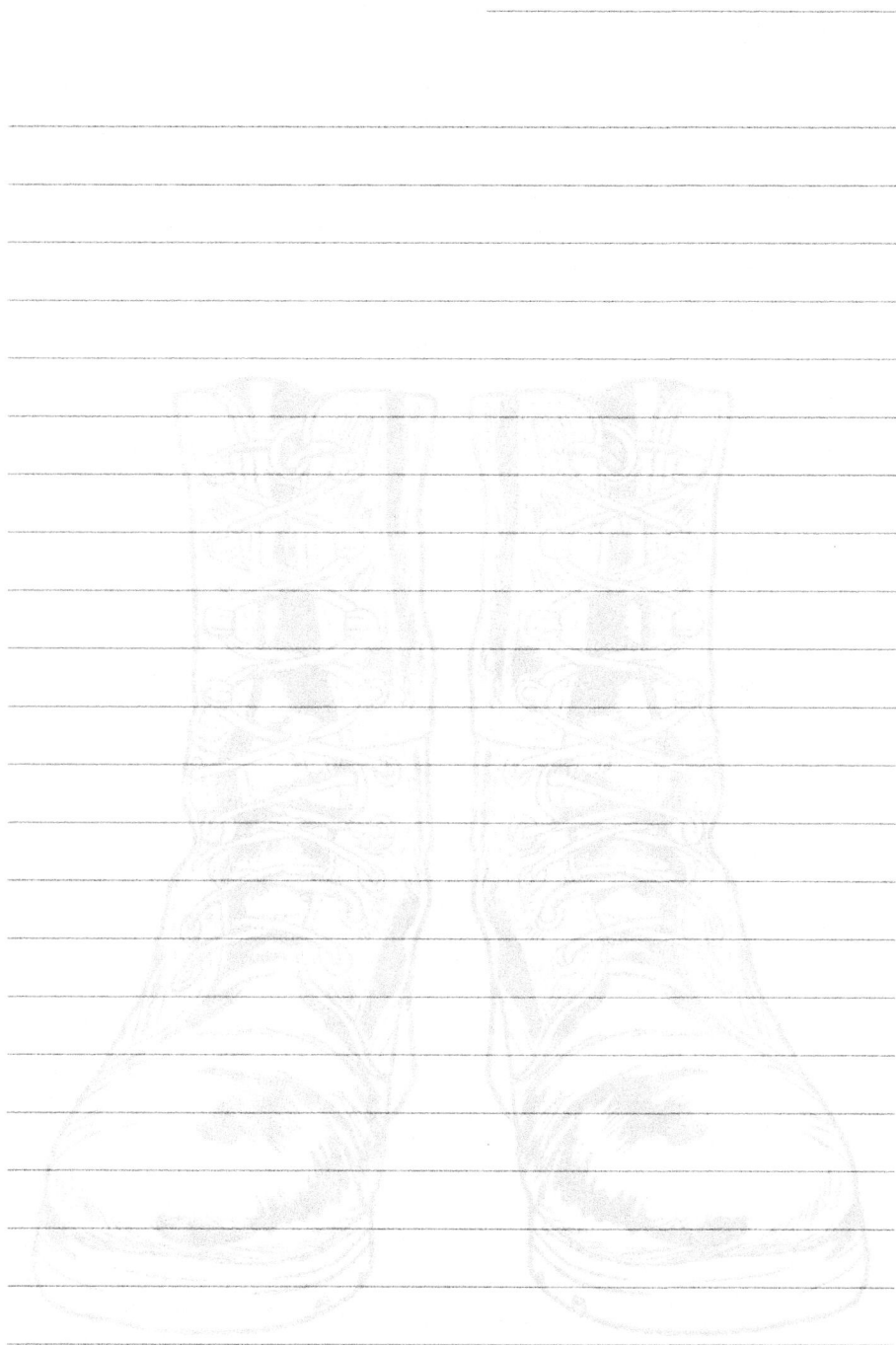

HAPPENINGS

_____
_____
_____
_____
_____
_____
_____
_____

EXPERIENCES

_____
_____
_____
_____
_____
_____

THOUGHTS

_____
_____
_____
_____
_____
_____
_____
_____

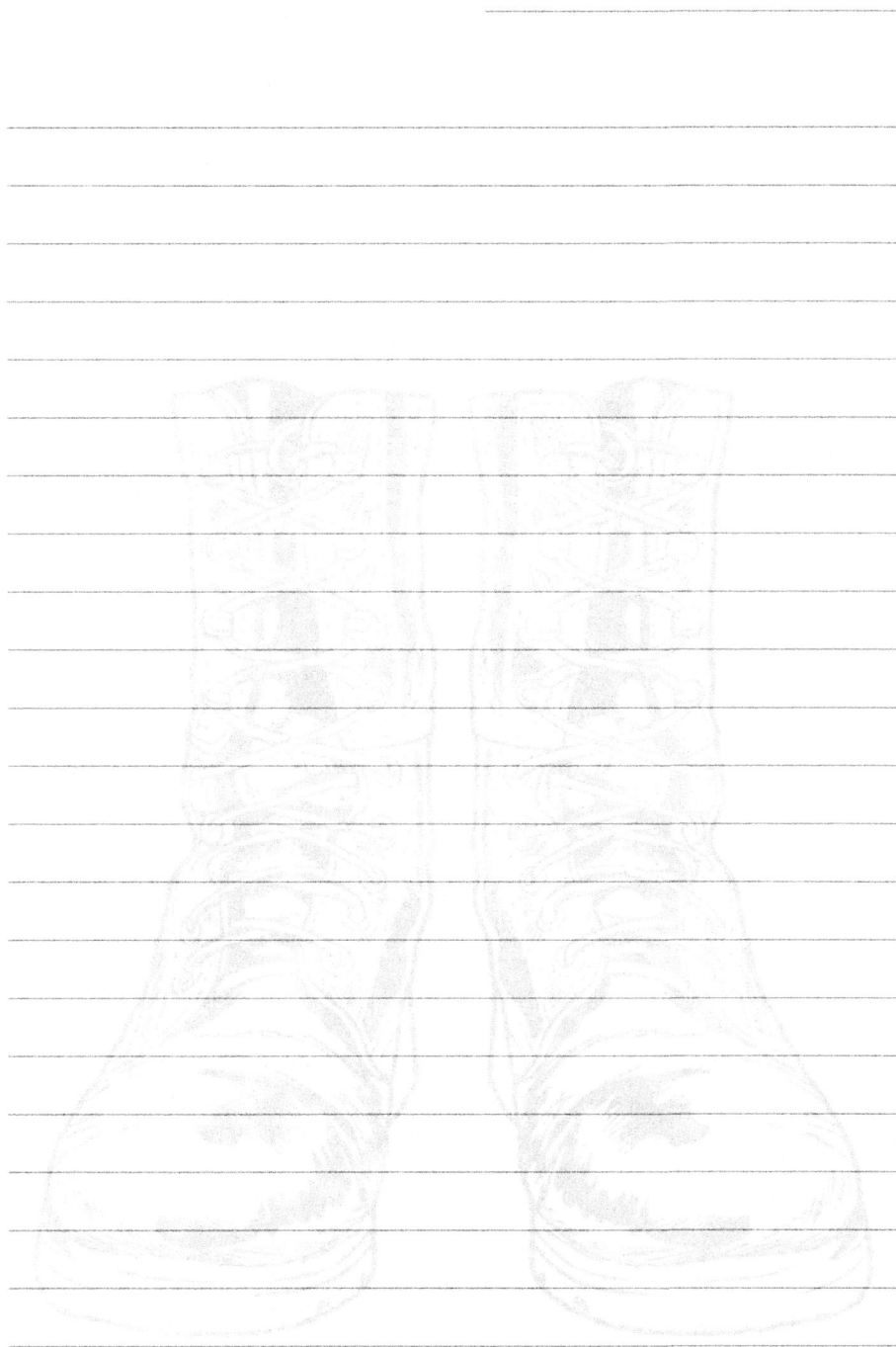

HAPPENINGS

EXPERIENCES

THOUGHTS

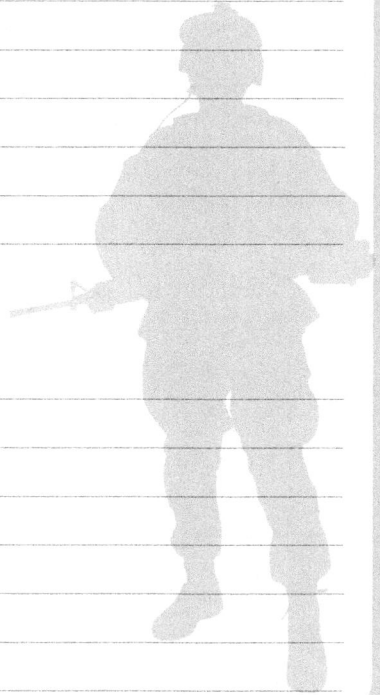

HAPPENINGS

EXPERIENCES

THOUGHTS

CONTACTS:

name: _____
address: _____
email: _____
phone: _____

name: _____
address: _____
email: _____
phone: _____

name: _____
address: _____
email: _____
phone: _____

name: _____
address: _____
email: _____
phone: _____

name: _____
address: _____
email: _____
phone: _____

name: _____
address: _____
email: _____
phone: _____

CONTACTS:

name: _____
address: _____
email: _____
phone: _____

name: _____
address: _____
email: _____
phone: _____

name: _____
address: _____
email: _____
phone: _____

name: _____
address: _____
email: _____
phone: _____

name: _____
address: _____
email: _____
phone: _____

name: _____
address: _____
email: _____
phone: _____

CONTACTS:

name: _____
address: _____
email: _____
phone: _____

name: _____
address: _____
email: _____
phone: _____

name: _____
address: _____
email: _____
phone: _____

name: _____
address: _____
email: _____
phone: _____

name: _____
address: _____
email: _____
phone: _____

name: _____
address: _____
email: _____
phone: _____

CONTACTS:

name: _____
address: _____
email: _____
phone: _____

name: _____
address: _____
email: _____
phone: _____

name: _____
address: _____
email: _____
phone: _____

name: _____
address: _____
email: _____
phone: _____

name: _____
address: _____
email: _____
phone: _____

name: _____
address: _____
email: _____
phone: _____

CONTACTS:

name: _____
address: _____
email: _____
phone: _____

name: _____
address: _____
email: _____
phone: _____

name: _____
address: _____
email: _____
phone: _____

name: _____
address: _____
email: _____
phone: _____

name: _____
address: _____
email: _____
phone: _____

name: _____
address: _____
email: _____
phone: _____

CONTACTS:

name: _____
address: _____
email: _____
phone: _____

name: _____
address: _____
email: _____
phone: _____

name: _____
address: _____
email: _____
phone: _____

name: _____
address: _____
email: _____
phone: _____

name: _____
address: _____
email: _____
phone: _____

name: _____
address: _____
email: _____
phone: _____

CONTACTS:

name:

address:

email:

phone:

name:

address:

email:

phone:

name:

address:

email:

phone:

name:

address:

email:

phone:

name:

address:

email:

phone:

name:

address:

email:

phone:

CONTACTS:

name: _____
address: _____
email: _____
phone: _____

name: _____
address: _____
email: _____
phone: _____

name: _____
address: _____
email: _____
phone: _____

name: _____
address: _____
email: _____
phone: _____

name: _____
address: _____
email: _____
phone: _____

name: _____
address: _____
email: _____
phone: _____

CONTACTS:

name: _____
address: _____
email: _____
phone: _____

name: _____
address: _____
email: _____
phone: _____

name: _____
address: _____
email: _____
phone: _____

name: _____
address: _____
email: _____
phone: _____

name: _____
address: _____
email: _____
phone: _____

name: _____
address: _____
email: _____
phone: _____

CONTACTS:

name: _____
address: _____
email: _____
phone: _____

name: _____
address: _____
email: _____
phone: _____

name: _____
address: _____
email: _____
phone: _____

name: _____
address: _____
email: _____
phone: _____

name: _____
address: _____
email: _____
phone: _____

name: _____
address: _____
email: _____
phone: _____

Made in the USA
Las Vegas, NV
18 May 2025

22337650R00128